14
17
21
mf
25
28

32
35
38
42
rit. poco a poco
46
mp
molto rit. e dim.
p

(Approx. Performance Time – 3:15)

One Thing Remains
(Your Love Never Fails)

But God demonstrates his own love for us in this:
While we were still sinners, Christ died for us.

—Romans 5:8 (NIV)

Words and Music by Jeremy Riddle,
Brian Johnson, and Christa Black
Arr. Carol Tornquist

11
14
to Coda
a tempo
poco rit.
17
20
22

24
p
mf
27
30
D.S. al Coda
mp
Coda
a tempo
rit.
36
molto rit. e dim.
p

(Approx. Performance Time – 3:15)

HOW HE LOVES

For God so loved the world that he gave his one and only Son,
that whoever believes in him shall not perish but have eternal life.

—John 3:16 (NIV)

Words and Music by
John Mark McMillan
Arr. Carol Tornquist

Flowing (♩. = 52)

17
21
25
29
34
f
mf

38
42
46
50
a tempo
poco rit.
54